African Grey Parrots

...getting started

by Helmut Pinter

Contents

Originally published in German by Franckh'sche Verlagshandlung, W. Keller & Co., Stuttgart under the title *Unser Graupapagei.* © 1985 by Franckh'sche Verlagshandlung, W. Keller & Co.

© T.F.H. Publications, Inc.

Distributed in the UNITED STATES to the Pet Trade by T.F.H. Publications, Inc., 1 TFH Plaza, Neptune City, NJ 07753; on the Internet at www.tfh.com; in CANADA by Rolf C. Hagen Inc., 3225 Sartelon St., Montreal, Quebec H4R 1E8; Pet Trade by H & L Pet Supplies Inc., 27 Kingston Crescent, Kitchener, Ontario N2B 2T6; in ENGLAND by T.F.H. Publications, PO Box 74, Havant PO9 5TT; in AUSTRALIA AND THE SOUTH PACIFIC by T.F.H. (Australia), Pty. Ltd., Box 149, Brookvale 2100 N.S.W., Australia; in NEW ZEALAND by Brooklands Aquarium Ltd., 5 McGiven Drive, New Plymouth, RD1 New Zealand; in SOUTH AFRICA by Rolf C. Hagen S.A. (PTY.) LTD., P.O. Box 201199, Durban North 4016, South Africa; in JAPAN by T.F.H. Publications, Japan—Jiro Tsuda, 10-12-3 Ohjidai, Sakura, Chiba 285, Japan. Published by T.F.H. Publications, Inc.

MANUFACTURED IN THE
UNITED STATES OF AMERICA
BY T.F.H. PUBLICATIONS, INC.

Introduction

DESCRIPTION OF THE GENUS

One of the oldest descriptions of the Grey Parrot in an animal book was written by the Swiss naturalist Konrad Gesner (1516 – 1565): "I also have one that is ash-colored or light blue over its whole body, except on the tail alone it has red feathers, and around the eyes it is white." Today, in the genus of the Grey Parrot (*Psittacus*), one species

(*Psittacus erithacus* Linne, 1758) and two subspecies are recognized: *Psittacus erithacus erithacus* Linne, 1758 and *Psittacus erithacus timneh* Fraser, 1884. At one time the Grey Parrots that lived on the islands of Principe and Fernando Po were considered to be a separate subspecies (*Psittacus erithacus princeps*). Because they differ very little from the parrots of the mainland, their

subspecific status is recognized by relatively few ornithologists.

1. Grey Parrot, nominate form (*Psittacus erithacus erithacus* Linne, 1758)

Body Length: 32 to 37 centimeters. Wing length: 22 to 25 centimeters. Tail length: 8.5 to 9.5 centimeters. If one compares the measurements of body length and wing length in a large number of individuals of both sexes, it will be shown statistically that

The upper mandible of the nominate form is solid black. The Timneh Grey Parrot has a reddish-gray to pink colored mandible. Photo by Isabelle Francais.

males have a somewhat greater body and wing length. The differences are so slight, however, that they are of no value as a sex characteristic.

The ground color is slate to light gray. The feathers on the neck and head are grayish white, with mostly dark edging. The bare cere at the base of

the bill and the bare eye ring are grayish white. The rump feathers are a distinctly lighter gray than the back feathers. The tail feathers are bright red. The bill is black and the legs are gray. The iris is grayish black in youngsters up to about the fifth to seventh month of life, and then gradually changes

color to a light gray. Only over the course of the following two to three years does the iris take on its ultimate coloration. This is always light, but can vary in tint. Usually it is a light yellowish white; however, birds with a grayish white iris lacking any yellow tinge are also found. Before their first molt, youngsters have a darker plumage of a light grayish-brown shade.

2. Timneh Grey Parrot (*Psittacus erithacus timneh* Fraser, 1844)

Body Length: 30 to 32 centimeters. Wing length: 20 to 22.5 centimeters. Tail length: 8 to 9 centimeters. The color of the plumage is dark gray over the entire body,

Opposite: The nominate form also differs from the Timneh Grey Parrot in size. It has a slightly larger and stockier build than the Timneh. Photo by Michael Defreitas.

including the wings. On different parts of the body, however, the same grades of coloration as in the nominate form are recognizable. As a rule, the feathers have distinct feather edging only on the breast and belly. The tail feathers are reddish brown to dark wine red. In youngsters, the tail feathers are more grayish brown. The upper mandible is pink at the base and darker toward the tip. Coloring and

differences in coloration of the iris in both youngsters and adults are the same as in the nominate form.

GEOGRAPHIC DISTRIBUTION, SUBSPECIES, AND VARIETIES

The homeland of the Grey Parrot is tropical Africa, approximately from Sierra Leone and Guinea in the west to Uganda, northwestern Tanzania, and southwestern Kenya in the east. In the north, the range

Right: The feathers on the head and breast of the Grey have a distinct edging creating a scalloped or laced appearance. Photo by Joan Balzarini.

extends to a latitude of about ten degrees. Although the Grey Parrot has very few subspecies, the large living space is populated by birds characterized by many different colors, nuances, and sizes. Birds that come from the rain forest or higher elevations exhibit a darker plumage than those from the savanna or

In the past, the principle enemy of the Grey Parrot was man. Birds were killed to be eaten as food and also for their bright red tail feathers. Photo courtesy of Vogelpark Walsrode.

cultivated areas. For this reason, it is assumed that the color varieties are in part determined by climatic conditions and diet. With a bird kept in captivity, the ground color may also change over the years; that is, originally light birds may become darker, or the reverse.

The Timneh Grey Parrot subspecies (*Psittacus erithacus timneh*), is easily distinguished from the nominate form by two typical characteristics. Whereas in the "normal" Grey Parrot both the upper and lower mandibles are black, in the Timneh Grey Parrot the base of the upper mandible is reddish gray to pink. The other difference is that the tail feathers of the nominate form are bright red, and those of the Timneh Grey Parrot are reddish brown. In addition, the Timneh Grey Parrot may also be somewhat smaller and have darker plumage. The range of the subspecies *Psittacus erithacus timneh* is limited to southern Guinea, Sierra Leone, and Liberia, where it primarily occurs near the coast. The term "Timneh" is derived from "Timmani," which is the name of a group of peoples indigenous to the region.

WILD GREY PARROTS AND THEIR LIVING CONDITIONS

In a report from the years 1872 to 1873, Dr. A. Reichenow wrote that Grey Parrots were so abundant in West Africa in the previous century that they

The name *"timneh"* was derived from the inhabitants of Sierra Leone. One of the tribes found there is the "Timmani." Photo by Robert Pearcy.

Parrots are generally social birds; they live in feeding flocks and nest in trees. Photo by Michael Defreitas.

All parrots like to chew. The Grey Parrot is no exception to this. Natural branches may be used as chew toys providing they are not treated with insecticides or pesticides and are not otherwise toxic. Photo by Michael Gilroy.

were considered to be an affliction in some areas. Reichenow writes: "No matter which way one turns, one is followed every-where by the screech-ing of the *Jakos* (common name for Grey Parrot). Old and young birds form flocks after the nesting season, which wander about in search of food and roosts. For the night they choose the highest trees as roosts, on which they gather each evening. The number of birds that land in the crown of a large tree can amount to several hundred. The next morning they set out under a continuous strident outcry, and move inland accompanied by loud croaking and screeching in order to plunder the maize fields of the natives on the high plains. During the nesting season, which falls during the rainy months (thus at different times north and south of the equator), the pairs live more or less by themselves in the mangrove forests of the coastal zone. There, using their powerful bills, they hollow out existing cavities in the branches of trees to form suitable nest holes."

Reichenow further adds in his report: "One can truly describe the flight of the Grey Parrot as pitiful. With short, fast wingbeats they strive to reach

their goal in a straight line. In the process they look so timid, as if they were constantly afraid of falling."

In former times, the Grey Parrot was adapted to quite variable environmental and climatic conditions within its extensive range. Since then, large areas of the African environment have been subjected to severe disruption. Ruthless exploitation of the rain forests, burning and clearing of woodland, agricultural utilization, overgrazing of savannas, oil drilling, and the like have changed the original

Grey Parrots have a life span in excess of 50 years. It is important for prospective buyers to be aware of the lifelong commitment they will have with such a pet. Photo by Michael Gilroy.

Grey Parrots have very powerful bills; however, they are very delicate in their eating habits. Photo by Michael Gilroy.

landscape in many places. As a consequence, in some areas where Grey Parrots were once abundant, they have become rare or have even disappeared

In the past, Grey Parrots were captured out of nests by natives who would sell them to traders for very high prices. The destruction of their habitat (cutting down trees) drastically diminished the population. Photo by Joan Balzarini.

completely. At the northern limit of their original range in particular, where Grey Parrots were common 40 to 50 years ago, there is only savanna and desert today. Nevertheless, this species is by no means rare in certain parts of its living space, although it is not as common as it once was.

Wild Grey Parrots principally feed on various seeds, fruits, and berries. They set out in flocks from their roosting trees and travel about in search of food; for example, fields of half-ripe maize. Just as well-liked are the fruits of olive trees and nuts.

Whether birds in the wild also include food of animal origin in their diet has not been sufficiently studied, but apparently they do. Observations of newly captured adults have shown that these birds by no means reject animal food in the form of raw eggs or small vertebrates (for example, small lizards and nesting mice).

FROM THE RAIN FOREST TO CIVILIZATION

Formerly, steamers and sailing ships carried Grey Parrots from West Africa to Europe. The "sailing ship birds," despite the considerably longer journey, had a much better chance of surviving than the Grey Parrots that were transported in the suffocating holds of the

Birds eat all day long but take their main meal at night, filling their crops for their sleep. Photo by Michael Gilroy.

Natural branches and leaves simulate the life of the Grey in the wild. It is a good idea to offer these to a Grey Parrot that is kept in the home. Photo by Michael Gilroy.

It is dangerous to feed parrots irregularly. Their main meal should be fed at night time so that their crop is full during sleep. A varied diet is best. Photo by Michael Gilroy.

steamers. Moreover, at the end of the nineteenth century it was believed that the parrots should not be given water during the journey.

The combination of improper diet, the accommodations in the cramped, unventilated space, and the change in climate did much to increase the mortality rate of the captured animals.

Today parrots now reach Europe in 20 to 30 hours without difficulty by air-plane. But in contrast to the past, it is often significantly more difficult to obtain them in the exporting countries because in many places they are no longer found in the same numbers as they were at the turn of the century.

After their arrival, parrots are subject to a legal quarantine period in almost all European countries. In the Federal Republic of Germany and in Switzerland, for example, birds must be isolated for eight weeks in special quarantine areas, and in Austria, for four weeks. During this time, the imported parrots undergo a preventive treatment with tetracycline. Tetracycline is an antibiotic that is effective against the pathogens of so-called parrot fever (psittacosis or ornithosis).

At the end of the quarantine period, healthy birds receive an official foot band, on which a serial number is stamped. This legally prescribed band is the proof of legal importation, and

Quarantine periods are necessary for all birds that are imported. Newly acquired birds should be isolated for a period of time to check for any signs of illness and learn a little about their normal habits and character. Photo by Robert Pearcy.

should therefore not be removed except for a compelling reason. Federal regulations restrict the importation of many species of birds into the United States and has therefore made captive breeding become quite popular.

The difference in coloration among Greys is sometimes affected by altering the living conditions of the bird, such as changing its diet or climate. Photo by Joan Balzarini.

The Purchase

Before acquiring a Grey Parrot, one should by all means learn about the habits, keeping, and proper care of this bird.

Because Grey Parrots are by nature extremely social birds, which live together in flocks or in pairs, when keeping a single bird, the owner must take the place of others of its kind; that is, the owner of a Grey Parrot must have much time, patience, and an understanding of the bird's needs. A Grey Parrot left completely to itself day after day wastes away through boredom and sadness, no longer eats, is susceptible to infectious illnesses, or even pulls out its own feathers (feather plucking).

It is strongly recommended that, if the purchaser realizes he will not have the time necessary for the bird, but definitely wants to keep a Grey Parrot, he should either purchase or provide a playmate. The companion could be an Amazon Parrot, one of the smaller Cockatoos, or any parrot of a different species. Compatibility should be tested, because as a rule, Grey Parrots are individuals, each of which has its own temperament and must be treated differently. Talk to your pet shop dealer. Maybe the Grey Parrot you are considering has already found a "mate" in the shop.

Upon bringing the bird home, it should be left completely alone. The only thing one should do is give it food and water. Photo by Robert Pearcy.

AN ACQUISITION FOR LIFE

That Grey Parrots can live to be 100 years old is perhaps something of an exaggeration, but 50 and 60-year-olds, and even 80-year-olds are known. One must be fully aware that the life expectancy of a

weigh it. The bird is first weighed in the cage and then the cage is weighed separately. Depending on size, normally nourished Grey Parrots weigh between 320 and 550 grams. (10.25–17.5 oz.) Taking into account the size of the bird, not even a very small and delicate Grey Parrot should weigh less than 300 grams (9.5 oz.). Large, robust birds can weigh 500 to 550 grams (16–17.5 oz.), and, in exceptional cases, up to 600 grams (19.25 oz.).

The condition of the plumage is normally a good indication of the bird's general state of health. Grey Parrots that have damaged plumage, which looks somewhat plucked and thinned out, consists of broken feathers, or are dirty looking, are not cause to worry. One should never buy a parrot with bare spots in its plumage, such as on the neck or the breast. A bird of this kind could be a feather plucker, and

The feathers of the Grey Parrot are dense. It is important to occasionally check the body weight of the bird by feeling through the feathers to the breast bone. The breast bone should never protrude. Photo by Isabelle Francais.

feather plucking is a habit that is virtually impossible to break. A deceiving bird seller may be likely to palm off the feather plucker on an unsuspecting customer as a partially feathered youngster.

Birds are susceptible to catching colds if housed in drafty areas. One should make sure, that the nostrils are not gummed up and that the bird does not sneeze.

An examination of the candidate's eyes, bill, and feet before the purchase is essential. The rims of the eyes must be clean and free of scabby deposits and the eyes themselves must be clear and lively. The upper and lower mandibles should meet without a noticeable gap and must be straight when viewed from the front.

Erect edges of the scales of the feet could be an indication of an infestation of mange mites. Birds that have erect scale edges or even scabby deposits on the feet or the upper side of the toes should be examined by a veterinarian before the purchase.

The bird's droppings should be of a soft consistency, but in no way liquidy or frothy.

ACQUIRING AN ACCLIMATED GREY PARROT

With luck, it may be possible to buy a "second hand" Grey Parrot from a private source, and if one is really lucky, the seller will be more interested in knowing that the bird finds its way into good hands than he will in the price. Because of a change in family circumstances, an elderly couple gave a good-talking Grey Parrot to our zoo, which quickly became popular with the visitors and staff. The couple visited their bird regularly, at least once a week. Not only was the bird charming and good-natured, it also sang and whistled all kinds of drinking songs, which to the visitors' delight always ended with an emphatic "Bottoms up!" Moreover, it could mimic wonderfully the voice and accent of a very popular sports announcer, and, to the delight of visitors, it commented on football matches and other sporting

A wild caught Grey Parrot may be somewhat timid and will gradually need to be accustomed to you and its new surroundings. After a short time, attempt to feed the bird seeds and nuts from your hand. Photo by Michael Gilroy.

events. But after a rainy day with only a few visitors the parrot had disappeared. The aviary's lock apparently had been opened with a skeleton key and the parrot had been stolen. The theft was extremely distressing to the keepers, because what would they say to the previous owners when they came and asked about the bird? The problem was solved in a surprising way, for the elderly couple was never again seen in the zoo. Among the staff the realization dawned that the couple had taken the bird back home. After some deliberation, we decided to allow for extenuating circumstances and did not take any further action.

It is of course also possible to be swindled in a private purchase. I am familiar with a case from Sweden where, under the pretense of changed family circumstances, a good-talking Grey Parrot was sold for a relatively high price. This bird could imitate precisely the sound of a smoke alarm—and this in a country where most houses are built of wood!

Generally speaking, when buying a talking bird, there is the risk that it could have in its vocabulary a number of

undesirable expressions. In this regard, the talking and mimicking ability of the Grey Parrot is not dependent on sex. Some females are excellent talkers, and some males never learn a single word. The ideal parrot owner shows interest in and gives attention to his bird even if it does not develop into a good talker.

Also asking the parrot's previous owner whether the bird is a "man's bird" or a "woman's bird" is advisable. Well-acclimated Grey Parrots quite often prefer members of one sex and dislike members of the other. A bird of this kind may, for example, be very fond of women but dislike men intensely—or vice-versa.

THE AVIARY

For a bird that is as active and curious as the Grey Parrot, it is particularly important for it to be able to move about to its heart's content. An aviary is the spacious solution to this problem because the bird can satisfy its natural impulse for movement without flying away or causing damage in the house.

Aviaries are large flight cages, which are permanently installed either in the house or outdoors. All aviaries should have at least one solid side wall—better yet, two solid side walls—for protection against draft, rain, heat, and cold. Solid side walls provide nervous birds a certain feeling of security. The best location for an indoor aviary is a corner of a room. For the home construction of a fairly small indoor aviary, finished wire frames in the dimensions of 1 x 2 meters (3 x 6½ ft)—with or without doors—are available on the market. Aviaries on a balcony, in a courtyard, or in the garden should, if possible, also be built attached to a solid wall. If this is impossible, two sides should be composed of an opaque, windproof material. Outdoor flight cages are constructed

Grey Parrots will benefit from the spacious accommodations of an outdoor aviary. Photo by Louise Van der Meid.

Above: If planned correctly, both you and the birds will benefit from an aviary. Photo by David Alderton. **Right:** Your bird cage should be sprayed regularly with mite & lice spray to be sure they stay free of harmful parasites. Photo courtesy of Four Paws.

either on a concrete slab or on a concrete foundation, which should extend at least one meter into the ground or should rest on a rock substrate. This protects against the rats and mice that are attracted by the parrot feed, as well as predators such as foxes, raccoons, and weasels, which could otherwise find their way into the aviary.

All metal parts of the weight-bearing aviary structure and the wire must consist of galvanized, rust-free material. For the weight-bearing structure, either galvanized plumbing pipe or the somewhat more expensive

To keep your parrot healthy and happy and to prevent boredom, there are many accessories available to furnish the cage. Photo courtesy of The Kong Company.

rectangular pipe should be used. A practical material for the wire is spot-welded wire mesh with a heavy wire gauge. The wire mesh should be fastened together to the frame with strong galvanized tie wire. Plastic-coated wire mesh is not a suitable material, because the birds will bite through the plastic coating.

The door opening should be large enough so that one can comfortably enter the aviary through it. Two doors, one that may be closed behind you before opening the second, are advisable in very large flight cages and with a large number of birds so that no birds can escape. A net hung in front of the door

opening of the aviary is also practical, although this precautionary measure is seldom required when keeping a single Grey Parrot. If the plans are to keep or breed a fairly large number of Grey Parrots outdoors, the aviary should be provided with a heated shelter room.

The wire of an aviary used to house Grey Parrots should be of a heavy gauge so that the birds are not able to break it apart with their powerful beaks. Photo by Michael Gilroy.

It is quite important to equip all doors of parrot cages and indoor aviaries with secure locks. Grey Parrots find it very amusing to open even complicated locks. Often only a small padlock will help to keep your parrots behind bars.

THE CLIMBING TREE

A hardwood climbing tree is indispensable for your bird's exercise and gnawing inclination. If the bark and horizontal branches provide sufficient inducement to keep it occupied, then your furniture will also be spared. Because Grey Parrots are very lively and are easily thrown into panic if they are chained, keeping the bird on a climbing tree requires that the bird's wings be clipped. Thick branches or treetops of beech, ash, oak, and the like make suitable climbing trees. Knobby pine leaders are also a good material. If a climbing tree is used in conjunction with a normal wire cage, it will be possible to confine the bird overnight or when it must be left unattended. If the parrot is given a specific treat only while in the cage, then it usually will not be a problem to train it to go into the cage on demand.

Food bowls should be installed in a suitable place on the climbing tree.

The base of a beach umbrella, a Christmas tree stand, or a bucket filled with sand will prevent the climbing tree from tipping over.

Opposite: The branches used on a climbing tree should vary in diameter. This will provide the proper exercise for the bird's feet and help to keep the nails trim by naturally wearing them down as they touch the wood. Photo by Tom Caravagalia.

Food bowls can be installed somewhere on the climbing tree or they can be placed at the base to keep dropped food to a minimum. Photo by Michael Gilroy.

Proper Feeding

THE DIGESTIVE ORGANS

It becomes clear when watching large parrots eat that they are primarily seedeaters. The parrot's upper and lower mandible, together with the powerful tongue, which is equipped with erectile organs, form a perfect instrument for shelling and husking seeds of all kinds. Its mouth contains numerous salivary glands that produce a slippery

mucus, which makes the often dry food easier to swallow.

Food enters the crop through the short esophagus. In parrots this is made up of two crop sacs, of which the left one is always filled first when feeding.

Only when the left crop sac is filled is food also taken into the right side. For this reason, the crop is often more readily visible on the left side than on the right.

The crop, the site of the first step of digestion, is of great importance in food utilization. Even if the stomachs (parrots have two) are empty, the food stays in the crop for a certain amount of time. In the crop, the often hard seeds are mixed with saliva and drinking water and are caused to swell. Young birds are fed from their parents' crops with predigested food.

After leaving the crop, the food next enters the thin-walled proventriculus. This is an elastic sac without appreciable musculature, which can also serve for food storage. Its principal function, however, is the production of substances that are critical for the digestive process, such as pepsin, hydrochloric acid, and so forth. The glands of the

Above: The natural food of the Grey Parrot includes seeds, nuts, fruits, berries, and vegetables. Photo by Joan Balzarini.

Opposite: The food preferences of Grey Parrots are so strong that it is often difficult to convince the bird to accept a new food variety. Photo by Isabelle Francais.

proventriculus also produce a substance that protects the mucous membranes of the stomach from the caustic action of the digestive juices.

The food, which is now mixed with digestive enzymes, is transported from the proventriculus to

digestion are added. The bile ducts and the outlet of the pancreas empty into this part of the intestine. Parrots do not have a gall bladder.

Essential nutrients as well as water are absorbed through the intestinal mucous membrane. A

If a choice of foods are given, the Grey Parrot will eat its favorite first. Hopefully, the bird will have more than one favorite and will be able to have a well balanced and varied diet. Photo by Michael Gilroy.

the ventriculus. There the stomach walls, which consist of two powerful pairs of muscles, grind down the seeds. The pressure developed by the muscles of the ventriculus is so great that even nuts are ground up easily.

From the outlet of the ventriculus—the pylorus—the prepared food gradually enters the duodenum, where additional substances critical for

further extraction of water, which is associated with the final thickening of the droppings, takes place in the large intestine. The large intestine ultimately opens, as do the urinary and genital outlets, into the cloaca.

THE DAILY BREAD

As its daily bread, the Grey Parrot requires a variety of foods, including a high-quality seed mixture, fresh fruits and vegetables, as well as nutritious prepared foods and occasional favorite treats.

When putting together the seed mixture, it will be discovered that the parrot possesses quite individual tastes, which can also change from day to day just as people also have their favorite foods which they like to vary from time to time. Who wants to eat hamburgers and french fries day in and day out? It has also been determined that when keeping several parrots, food jealousy and the impulse to imitate increase the appetite inordinately and the most diverse kinds of foods are eaten.

We have included a table which provides information about the proportion of basic nutrients in various foods. With sunflower seeds and peanuts, the values given apply to kernels without shells, because with sunflower seeds in particular, the proportion of shell in the total weight can be quite variable. If a Grey Parrot completely

PROPORTION OF BASIC NUTRIENTS IN VARIOUS FOODS

	PERCENTAGE OF:			
	Raw fat	Raw protein	carbohydrate	ash
Sunflower seeds, shelled	54	20	6	2.7
Peanuts, shelled	41	26	11	2.4
Hemp	31	23	19	4.1
Oats	6.9	14.5	63	1.9
Wheat	1.8	11	73	1.7
Maize	4.1	9.5	70	1.6
Pumpkin seeds	35	26	5.6	3.7
Canary seed	5	15	53	4.1
Millet	4	12	60	3.5
Raw Rice	2.3	8.5	63	5.5
Apples	0.3	0.3	13.5	0.4
Pears	0.1	0.2	12.8	0.4
Bananas	0.6	1.5	29.6	1.0
Oranges	0.2	0.9	10.5	0.4
Grapes	—	0.3	9.4	0.5
Cherries	0.1	1.2	11.2	0.7
Plums	0.3	1.4	12.5	0.6
Carrots	0.2	1.2	9.4	1.0

If certain foods are completely rejected by the bird, something that is equal in nutritional value may be substituted. Graham crackers are often good substitutes. Photo by Joan Balzarini

refuses to eat particular seeds or fruits, it is often possible to substitute others of equivalent nutritional value.

The following applies to the other seeds listed in the table: peanuts are very nutritious and should be offered daily, but in moderation. Hemp seed should be fed, if at all, only in very small amounts. Hemp seed, which is grown in southern countries, possibly contains toxins that are injurious in the long run. Maize is an excellent food, particularly if still in a milky (half-ripe) state, which is liked by virtually all Grey Parrots. Fully ripened, hard kernels are not as well-liked. Pumpkin seeds are also readily eaten by some parrots. Millet can be added to the basic seed mixture, but is above all a treat in the form of spray millet. Raw rice is scarcely eaten in the hard state, although more often in sprouted form. The other seeds can also be fed occasionally in the sprouted state. Often the

bird will eat sprouted seeds that it ignored in the dry, hard state.

Nuts of all kinds, including sweet almonds, are a special treat for your pet. If you bring green hazelnuts back home from a walk in the country, your Grey Parrot will certainly prefer them to the ripe ones. Pine and spruce cones are coveted both as toys and as food; the bird can have fun tearing them apart and can also eat the seeds they contain.

A daily supplement of fruits and greens is also part of a complete diet. Offer your parrot small amounts of various fruits, vegetables, and sprouted seeds until you are familiar with its favorite foods and varying feeding habits. Besides juicy apples and pears, other fruits that can be fed include peaches, apricots, and grapes. All fruits must be thoroughly

washed and, if necessary, peeled before feeding to your bird. The pits of peaches, plums, and cherries are harmful because of the substances they contain and should be removed ahead of time. Grey Parrots also readily eat berries of various kinds, including strawberries, currants, whiteberries, blueberries, rowan berries, and raspberries. When feeding especially juicy pieces, however, do not forget that the table manners of the Grey Parrot come straight out of the jungle. Spattered juice and

Providing the Grey Parrot with the proper diet is extremely important.

empty berry hulls as well as fruit remains will soon decorate nearby walls, carpets, and the like. Grey Parrots kept singly in a cage will at times ignore fruit if it has fallen to the floor of the cage. To prevent this, pieces of apples, pears, and the like can be impaled on a blunt spike pointing diagonally upward.

Fresh twigs are also well-liked. The bird will enthusiastically gnaw off the buds and bark from them—less for the purpose of eating them than for the fun of it—to satisfy the need to gnaw; thus the climbing tree will be spared for a longer time. It goes without saying that no twigs from poisonous shrubs (viburnum, laburnum, and the like) or from trees treated with insecticides or fungicides should be used. Best-suited are fruit trees (except cherry), poplars, and willows.

Wild plants that can be given as greenfood include: chickweed, dandelion, clover, alfalfa, and plantain. Rosehips are also very readily eaten. Of the vegetables grown in the garden, lettuce and spinach are suitable.

A certain amount of animal protein also belongs in a healthy and balanced diet, for example: an occasional hard-boiled egg, a chicken bone to gnaw, or feed pellets, such as are used for puppies. In addition to food and fresh drinking water, your parrot must always have access to a cuttlebone or mineral block for the necessary minerals and calcium that it may not be receiving in its diet.

Parrot owners often ask the question: What can I give my parrot from the dinner table? On the condition that it is not carried to excess, one can give a healthy parrot almost anything. As a general principle, very salty and spicy foods should be avoided. Caution is also advisable when feeding cheese. Cheese is usually readily or even avidly eaten. For reasons that have not yet been explained though, a large amount of cheese may cause casein to

Opposite: Fresh twigs and bark not only satisfy the bird's need to gnaw, but it will consume certain buds and leaves. Use caution when offering these to your pet; certain household plants are poisonous. Photo by Robert Pearcy

Providing the Grey Parrot with the proper diet is extremely important. Photo courtesy of Hagen.

concentrate in the crop of some parrots, which can lead to serious digestive disturbances. To prevent this, feed only in moderation and in addition to the regular diet.

The best defense against possible deficiency symptoms is a balanced, varied diet. Although sunflower seeds are a very

Grey Parrots can be fed all types of people food in addition to their regular diet. Anything you can eat, the bird can eat, providing it is fed in moderation. Photo by Joan Balzarini.

nutritious food, a diet consisting exclusively of them is objectionable. Birds that are accustomed to the unbalanced feeding of sunflower seeds should have these completely excluded from the diet temporarily if they refuse to eat any other kinds of food. Nevertheless, with individual birds, it is often necessary to experiment for a long time before finding out what they like best. And you can run into the same problem that a young veterinarian experienced. After the proverb "A new broom sweeps clean," the new zoo veterinarian decided to test new foods, while the old Grey Parrots fought against him with all their might. It was decided that all large parrots were to be given dry dog food as a supplement. Two old Grey Parrots resolutely refused to eat the unfamiliar food, and they maintained their negative opinion even when starvation was used in an attempt to force them to eat. When the veterinarian asked one more time, "You mean you still haven't eaten the pellets?" one of the parrots joined in with the words, "You can eat them yourself." To what extent the animal keeper, who may not have had a particularly high opinion of the feeding experiments, lent a helping hand in this answer was never discovered.

DRINKING WATER

Make sure that your Grey always has fresh, clear drinking water

Opposite:
Grey Parrots cannot be sexed from their outward appearance. A veterinarian may perform certain procedures to determine the sex of your bird. Photo by Michael Defreitas.

available. If the water is soiled with food remains, droppings, and the like, the water must be changed several times a day, and the water bowl should always be clean. Birds that have been moved to a new environment should be given only spring water to drink at first. If the Grey Parrot eats a lot of greenfood and fruit in addition to its seeds, it will get enough vitamins. If it refuses "green stuff," a few drops of a vitamin preparation for large parrots can be added to its water bowl daily.

PURCHASING SEED

When buying seed, test all seeds that are very high in fat, such as sunflower seeds and nuts, by chewing a kernel to see if they are rancid. When premixed and packaged seed is stored at too high a temperature, pests like meal moths, mealworms, and others can infest it. For this reason, seed should only be bought in bulk or in transparent packages. To be on the safe side, all seeds should always be stored in the refrigerator or a cold storage chamber. Spoiled food is dangerous and should be disposed of.

Vitamin and mineral supplements can be placed on the bird's food. Powder forms are best for this type of administration. Photo courtesy of Hagen.

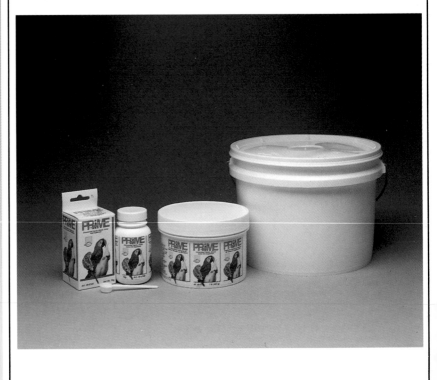

Acclimating

ACCLIMATING AND TAMING
It is best to bring your newly acquired pet home in a covered cage. So that the bird does not become frightened and is not subjected to draft, the cage should be wrapped in a wool blanket. Another possibility is transporting the bird in a cage with wire on only one side or in

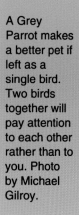

A Grey Parrot makes a better pet if left as a single bird. Two birds together will pay attention to each other rather than to you. Photo by Michael Gilroy.

a small box. Once the parrot arrives at home, it should be allowed to climb in its own cage, or one can attempt to coax it out.

Never take hold of the bird with your hand. Should this prove to be absolutely necessary, however, leave the task to an outsider.

Almost all Grey Parrots, even completely tame birds, have a panicky fear of gloves. All too often, they have had bad experiences with gloves and they resemble the human hand too much. If a large parrot must be held, a large, fluffy towel may be thrown over the bird. In any case, the bird should be prevented from associating this extremely unpleasant experience with its provider.

THE FIRST STEP

Have patience, and do not bother your new housemate more than is absolutely necessary during the first few days. In this way, it has the time and peace it needs to develop confidence in its immediate environment. Feeding, changing the water, and checking to see that it is eating are upsetting enough for the parrot—sudden events will leave it completely disconcerted.

After about a week, approach the cage slowly and carefully. In this effort, it will quickly become apparent where a particular bird's fear threshold lies. In this situation, untame birds attempt to press into a corner of the cage with their heads to the front and emit screeching cries. Older birds exhibit a flight

Grey Parrots frighten easily. Fast movements and loud noises are particularly bothersome to them. While attempting to train the bird, move slowly and speak softly to it. Photo by Michael Gilroy.

reaction or lean backward to avoid the intruder. Some even make desperate attempts to escape or try to bite their owner. How quickly the fear of people and mistrust are broken down depends on the particular bird. By way of exception, in the past, some wild-caught birds permitted themselves to be touched with the hand after only a few weeks; but it can also take months or even years to get this far. Only patience will lead to success. During the acclimatization process, the bird should be given fresh branches of poplar, willow, aspen, linden, elder, lilac, or fruit trees regularly. Branches for gnawing are an excellent form of occupational therapy for these active fellows. Even though

very little of the bark is consumed, the bird does obtain valuable minerals and trace elements in the portion it eats. Some Grey Parrots also like to play with toys. A length of thick chain, a hemp rope, or an old leather belt can serve the purpose. If a length of hemp rope is used, both ends of the rope must be secured with a tube clamp. Replace a chewed length of rope as soon as possible so that your bird does not become tangled in it.

Experience has shown that lively, alert birds that react to music and noises (for example, a vacuum cleaner) often turn out to be the best talkers. Nevertheless, avoid continuous noise, slamming doors, and disturbances in the beginning. If your bird reacts with loud and shrill screeches, then the cage

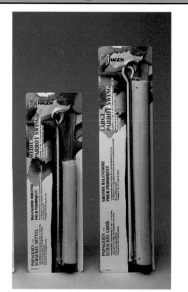

can occasionally be covered with a dark cloth. This dark cloth is sometimes helpful in curing some parrots of the habit of screeching. As soon as the bird starts to make noise, the cloth is placed over the cage and is left there for about thirty minutes. Whether or not this method will be successful depends on the particular Grey Parrot.

As soon as your new pet has become acclimated to

Parrot swings come in a variety of sizes for all types of birds and bird cages. Your local pet shop will carry all the different varieties so that you can choose one to suit your needs as well as the birds. Photo courtesy of Hagen.

Greys are infrequent bathers and do not like to be sprayed with water. Occasionally a Grey Parrot will attempt to take a bath in its water bowl. You may wish to supply a heavy, shallow dish on the floor for this. Photo by Michael Defreitas.

its new environment and is no longer thrown into panic when you approach the cage, hand taming may begin. Because your Grey Parrot should learn to climb up on the hand and to perch on the arm and shoulder, try to make this palatable in the following manner: first place the bird, whose wings must be clipped, on the floor. Grey Parrots feel extremely insecure on the ground, and use the first opportunity offered to them to climb up to a higher point. Hold a round stick about 1.5 meters long in front of the parrot's feet, so that the bird can climb onto it. Once the parrot is perched on the stick, lift it up. When the bird has gotten used to climbing on

a stick held in front of it, gradually reduce the distance between your hand and the bird. Once the bird realizes that the whole affair is not so dangerous after all, it is only a small step from the stick to the hand. In order to induce the bird to take this small step, pull the stick slowly with the free hand through the hand holding it, so that the length of stick on which the bird is perched becomes shorter and shorter. The bird will finally have no choice but to climb on the hand. As in all taming efforts, the degree of success is in proportion to the provider's patience and understanding of the bird's needs.

No matter how tame your parrot may seem to be,

Opposite: Grey Parrots become bored if left alone for long periods during the day. You may wish to consider purchasing an Amazon Parrot or other type of bird to keep the Grey company while you are away. Photo by Robert Pearcy.

Left: Fruits and vegetables are extra special treats that can be fed to your bird on a daily basis in addition to its regular diet. Photo by Michael Defreitas.

During preening the bird may spend as much as 15 minutes cleaning off dust, dirt, and loose down. Photo by Michael Gilroy.

The most suitable site for a parrot cage is a well lighted corner of the room that is free from drafts. Photo by Michael Gilroy.

there is no guarantee that the bird will not fly away if given the opportunity. Therefore, it is of the greatest importance to continually inspect the condition of the flight feathers of all large parrots kept at liberty. Even if it is usually possible to catch escaped birds, this can require a great deal of patience and cause a lot of agitation. Not to mention that the runaway will be exposed to all kinds of dangers.

Once it understands that your hands do not represent a threat, it will certainly permit you to scratch the back of its head and nape through the bars of the cage after a while. Avoid touching other parts of the body and any direct handling or even holding, because these are tolerated only by completely tame birds.

Whether or not one covers the bird cage overnight with a cloth must be decided from case to

case. On the one hand, if the cage is covered for a fairly long time, the material prevents circulation between the air in the cage

and in the room, and the bird receives too little oxygen. On the other hand, Grey Parrots can easily become frightened at twilight by sudden light, such as that of automobile headlights, and can injure themselves through aimless fluttering around. Grey Parrots see very poorly in semi-darkness, and can barely make out objects. For this reason, it is always better to cover the cage at night if disturbances are likely.

THE RUN OF THE HOUSE

As soon as your Grey Parrot feels secure behind the bars of its wire castle, and has otherwise completely lost its fear of the once unfamiliar environment, it may leave its cage. Open the door of

Left: Soon after the Grey Parrot loses its fear of the environment it becomes a master of its world. Greys become confident in their surroundings and begin to explore other nearby areas. Photo by Robert Pearcy.

the cage and let it stand open. If it has not ventured across the threshold after a short time, try to build a "bridge" for it. A long round stick—a broom handle, for example—stuck through the entrance hole makes it possible for the bird to leave the cage or climb up to the roof of the cage. If it lands on the floor on its first excursion, let it walk around undisturbed for a while. Then place the cage on the floor so it can climb in if it wants.

If you suspect that your new housemate is starting to develop somewhat more confidence when leaving the cage, make sure that it can recognize the windowpanes in the room as obstacles. Draw the curtains or place an object, such as a plant, in front of the window.

Opposite: To keep your bird from leaving its outside play area, occupy it with colorful toys and gnawing material. Photo by Michael Gilroy.

Care

An acclimated Grey Parrot, despite the warm climate of its homeland, is in no way delicate in regard to temperature, and does not need to be kept particularly warm. A room temperature of 18°–20° C (65–68°F) is completely adequate. Well-acclimated Grey Parrots that are kept in outdoor aviaries can stay there in the fall until the first night frosts. Caution is advised with changes in climate with newly acquired birds; they should be acclimated very carefully. In addition, all Greys are extremely sensitive to draft, which should be taken into account when installing cages, climbing trees, and indoor aviaries.

THE PLUMAGE

Normally, birds oil their plumage with an oily substance from the preen gland. In parrots, this gland is greatly reduced. Instead, they have numerous powder-down feathers, which keep the plumage soft and water-repellent. These feathers produce a powder that is visible as a grayish white dust on the plumage. If the bird shakes itself, this deposit rises up and covers the

surroundings with a fine white powder. In the wild, it is washed off from time to time by rain showers. If your pet is already completely tame, it will enjoy being taken into the bathroom and rinsed under the shower. However, if

your bird is still quite timid, you must not frighten it. Fill a sprayer, such as one used for the care of house plants, and carefully spray the bird with it. It will quickly become apparent whether it likes this or not. Some Grey Parrots splash directly in shallow water, while others bathe in sand, like chickens.

CLIPPING THE WINGS

As soon as the bird is more acclimated with its provider and its environment, it may leave the cage. Because a parrot in possession of its full flying ability can cause much mischief in a house, its wings should be clipped beforehand. Exceptions are birds that are kept in aviaries, and of course

An unsupervised bird can get into mischief. It is advisable to keep the wing of your Grey Parrot clipped so that it does not wander to places that are difficult for you to get it down from. Photo by Robert Pearcy.

those that will be used for breeding attempts.

The feathers are clipped of one or both wings. Birds with only one clipped wing cannot maintain their balance if they attempt to fly; instead, they tumble over and fall to the floor. If you have clipped your Grey Parrot's wings as prescribed, it will land on the floor after a brief, diagonal, fluttering flight a few meters from the starting point. Because clipped flight feathers grow back again, they must be inspected twice a year and feathers that have grown back must be clipped.

A person who is unfamiliar to the bird should perform the wing clipping. Then the Grey Parrot will not associate this unpleasant experience with the people in its environment. Only with completely tame birds should the provider clip the wings himself. While he plays with the bird, he can gradually cut away the appropriate feathers with a short, sturdy pair of scissors. If you are lacking in experience, turn to a reputable pet shop manager or a competent veterinarian.

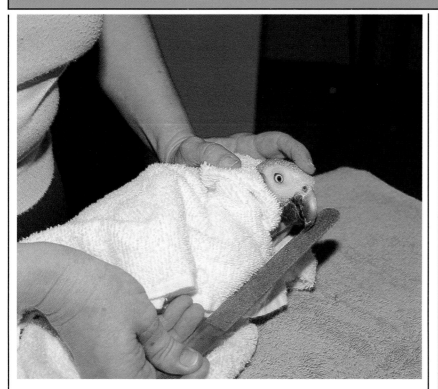

A reputable pet shop or a veterinarian can demonstrate the proper way to clip your bird's wing, beak, and claws. Photo by Louise Van der Meid.

CLAW AND BILL CARE

If the perches in the cage and on the climbing tree are adjusted to the size of the Grey Parrot, the bird's claws will seldom grow overly long. The best solution is to use branches and perches of various sizes, but always so large that the bird's foot cannot reach all the way around them. Squared perches that are rounded only on the corners have also proved to be effective. With sufficiently thick perching provisions, the tip of the claw always touches wood and is used in a natural manner. A balanced relationship of growth and wearing as well as the varying thicknesses of the perches serve to keep your parrot's feet flexible and its nails trim.

If claws must be clipped, then use clippers such as those used for clipping dogs' claws. The position of the blood vessel (pulpa) located in the claw can not easily be seen. Caution should be exercised. Should bleeding occur despite all caution when clipping the claws, it can easily be stopped by the use of a styptic powder available at most pet shops.

Abnormal bill growth or bill deformities are quite rare with Grey Parrots. Bill clipping or any other bill

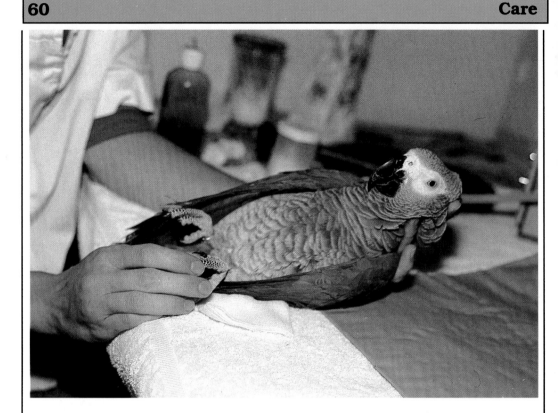

treatment should definitely be left to a veterinarian who has experience with birds.

HYGIENE

When buying the cage, make sure that it is easy to clean. With smaller cages, the bottom drawer is taken out daily, the droppings are removed with a small shovel, and sand or shavings should be spread on the soiled areas.

Depending on how soiled it is, the cage is given a thorough cleaning every two to three weeks. In the process, the bottom part and the perches should be scalded with boiling water. The climbing tree should also be treated in this fashion, although it is often easier to replace it. Of course, food and water bowls must also be rinsed out with clean water before every new meal.

A clean kept, well fed bird will have bright eyes and a healthy overall plumage. Photo by Isabelle Francais.

Behavior

TAMING

When discussing tame parrots, there must be a distinction between wild-caught birds, which have become acclimated to people over a certain period of time, and hand-reared birds, whose tameness is the result of false imprinting. In the latter case, the parrot is taken from the nest cavity early, and considers people to be others of its own kind.

Young birds become tame more quickly than adults, and it is said that females are more wary and cautious than males.

A trusting relationship, develops over time, and is usually limited to a particular person; the Grey Parrot stands aloof from other people. Because Grey Parrots are monogamous for life, you must expect a tame bird to eventually consider you to be its "mate," and for it to attempt to feed you from its crop with regurgitated food, for example. That male

parrots prefer women and female parrots prefer men is an old wives' tale, however, bird's do become favorable toward one sex.

DAY-TO-DAY BEHAVIOR

Observe your Grey Parrot on some occasion when it is taking a nap: perched on one leg, with somewhat ruffled plumage, it looks like a rotund, cuddly shuttlecock. After its nap it feels refreshed and venturesome. It stretches, spreads its tail feathers and wings. At this point, it usually waddles over to you to have its head scratched, or tries to draw attention to itself in some other manner. Marching through the room, it walks pigeon-toed. If it now holds out its head, then scratch it on the nape carefully with one or two fingers. If several birds live together, they often will preen and groom each other reciprocally (social grooming). If your Grey Parrot has had enough stroking and play, let it have its way. Perhaps it now wants to fluff up a little and doze in front of

A thorough grooming includes the bird's nails as well as each individual feather. Grey Parrots will sit for hours grooming themselves. Photo by Michael Gilroy.

you, or it is now time for the daily, thorough grooming. In so doing, it works through the underflue and lesser feathers with its bill and then cranes its neck with comical movements in order to arrange the wing and tail feathers.

The easiest way to become familiar with your pet's eating habits is to give your Grey Parrot a fairly

During the taming process a Grey Parrot will try to escape until it learns to trust you. Photo by Joan Balzarini.

large piece of food: first it takes the treat in its hand (foot), which will allow you to determine whether it is a pronounced "right- or left-hander." The offering will be appraised at bill level, and if the gift is acceptable, it will begin eating. Do not be surprised if only the seeds from an offered grape or a piece of apple are eaten. Grey Parrots are "spendthrifts," and recognize the difference between edible luxury articles and toys. The interplay of feet and bill is also apparent in climbing. Here the bill is used as a lifting and pulling instrument in support of the "leg work." A peculiar trait is knocking. The bird knocks hard with its bill against a solid object, such as a perch. The significance of this behavior is not known.

Grey Parrots also exhibit quite childish behavioral patterns. If you hold something in your hands, it will immediately also want to have it. A Grey Parrot that lived in the home of a

The full attention of a Grey Parrot is needed during taming. Photo by Joan Balzarini.

The Grey Parrot has the capacity to learn a great number of words and phrases. Photo by Robert Pearcy.

friend of mine had mastered only a few words, but was extraordinarily playful. This bird could play for hours with spools of thread, Ping-Pong balls, small tin cans, and the like by rolling them back and forth. Another of its passions was playing cards, a special liking that got the parrot in a little trouble. Each Wednesday evening, its owner had an appointment with several friends to play bridge. At first, the bird had followed the play perched on its owner's shoulder and had occasionally also put in one of its few words, which, by the way, were all derived from the card vocabulary. Everything was fine until the day it took a playing card from the table—at first apparently out of curiosity—and laid it on top of a cabinet. So a chair was placed in front of the

cabinet and the card was retrieved. But after this modest beginning, this was no longer so easy to do, because the parrot had learned. If a hand now reached for a stolen card, the bird picked it up in its bill again and carried it off to another place. The house was in an uproar as the card hunt continued. Moreover, the cards had now also been "marked" by the bird's beak. This led to "cage arrest" for the Grey Parrot once a week.

TALKING GREY PARROTS

Most people who acquire a single Grey Parrot as a house pet hope that the purchased bird will become a good talker. To guard against disappointments, it should be mentioned that by no means are all Grey Parrots gifted mimics. Most of them, to be sure, learn a few words and also reproduce these with astonishing fidelity of tone, but they never get beyond a small vocabulary. Others imitate sounds in their environment, mimic animal voices, or whistle melodies, but never say a human

word. Some, however, develop into true "talking geniuses" that effortlessly use several hundred words and often produce complete sentences. Such birds generally do not stop at talking, but, on the contrary, mimic all imaginable sounds they hear, such as the ringing of a telephone, barking

dogs, squeaking doors, and so forth. An owner of a Grey Parrot I am acquainted with reported that a kitchen faucet dripped for several days, and the falling drops produced a characteristic sound. After a few days the plumber came and repaired the damage. This stopped the dripping—not, however, the associated sound. The lady assured me that since that time the "faucet" still

When a bird talks it is imitating the speaker and most likely has no comprehension of the words unless associated with particular objects or actions. Photo by Michael Gilroy.

Greys are affectionate, long-lived, and their speaking ability is astonishing. Photo by Michael Gilroy.

caution is advised in what is said, because good talking parrots reveal a lot about the home environment of their family.

The fact that a talking parrot often makes appropriate comments about the events around it has given rise to many misinterpretations. It does, however, look as if the bird knows what it is saying. In reality, its commentary always follows after a specific word, sound, or event. A simple example is a parrot that says "hello" when the phone rings. It has learned that the word "hello" must follow the ringing of the telephone. The telephone bell is the cue for the word "hello." The bird responds with its commentary to a sound, to an "acoustic cue."

A simple example of a "visual cue" is if your parrot says "good night" as soon as it sees the black cloth which is used to cover its cage in the evening. It has already heard the words "good night" many times before in the same situation. It does not bother the bird in the least if it is broad daylight, because for it the black cloth and "good night" belong together just like

Toys should be absent from the cage when attempting to teach the Grey to talk. All of the bird's attention should be placed on you rather than on other objects. Photo by Michael Gilroy.

the previously mentioned ringing telephone and the word "hello."

Occasionally, a question-and-answer game of this kind can be carried to the highest level of perfection with performing Grey Parrots and their handlers. Be aware, however, that even with an unusually talented parrot, it is scarcely possible to achieve a similar result. The performance of the parrot and its demonstrator on stage is the result of a long, systematic education, in which a question posed by the keeper is the cue for a specific answer from the parrot. In addition, training of this kind requires that during the rehearsal time all other sounds are eliminated. Birds kept in homes, as good as they might be at talking, will always learn odds and ends from their environment between their studies. A Grey Parrot that could talk very well lived in the author's

family for many years. This bird, in the event that nothing appropriate happened for it, provided its own cause for commentary. If the dachshund that lived in the house barked because someone was ringing the doorbell, the bird often said in the wife's voice, "Be quiet and go in the kitchen." Normally, the typical course of events was as follows: the doorbell rang— the dachshund barked— the wife sent the dachshund in the kitchen. But if it was quiet for a long time during the day, and nobody rang the doorbell, the dachshund did not bark, the parrot found it to be much too boring. The bird's solution was to stage the whole thing itself. That is, first the doorbell

A Grey Parrot will "practice" while you are not present. A number of gurgling sounds and squeals will be attempted to be put together to repeat a desired sound. Photo by Michael Gilroy.

A favorite food may be given to the Grey as a reward for repeating a desired sound. Photo by Michael Gilroy.

The training process should not be too long. Grey Parrots will only become confused and over tired and will not retain any of the training in such a state. Photo by Michael Gilroy.

rang—the dachshund barked—and finally the wife bellowed, "Be quiet and go in the kitchen."

Many times I pronounced a phrase, "Scratch the nice bird's head," for this bird. It managed to imitate these words after a few weeks. If I now heard, "Scratch the nice bird's head," I stroked its head, which it greatly appreciated. Some time later it had learned to bow its head forward invitingly before saying, "Scratch the nice bird's head." It could, therefore, foresee the ensuing action, which after all does require a certain acumen. That this bird also learned to associate the appropriate sounds with many things that went on in the house is shown in the following examples. If a person reached for the water jug in order to water the house plants, then, before the jug was touched, the water could be heard gurgling. If someone put on their coat, a "goodbye" rang out. The bird could

perfectly imitate the voices of all four family members, which led to many misunderstandings. For example: "Why don't you answer when I call?"..."Oh, excuse me. I thought it was the parrot." Or also the reverse: "What's the matter?"..."I didn't call. That was the parrot." When the bird had its very quiet introspective periods, it peacefully philosophized away. In this way, entire telephone conversations it had learned could be followed in which throat clearing and pauses were interspersed between words, just as the bird had grasped them. In particular, telephone conversations that were frequently repeated in a similar form were to its liking; for example, the ordering of a pizza to be delivered: "Hm, hm...One large pie with extra cheese...hm, hm...to be delivered...Yes, please....Yes. Thank you. That is all."

Grey Parrots choose the highest possible place to perch, roost, and rest. Photo by Michael Defreitas.

parrot must first hear what it is supposed to say. Pronounce the desired words slowly and clearly for the bird. If a newly acquired bird shows no reaction at all to what is said and makes absolutely no attempt for weeks or even months to mimic them, provide yourself with a lot of patience and do not give up. With a new arrival that from the start whistles, screeches, and produces more or less articulate sounds, it is possible that it will quite suddenly produce a clearly spoken word.

Learning to talk is simplified with the aid of an ordinary cassette recorder. Record the desired words on the tape, check to see that no incidental noises can be heard, and then play the recording several times a day. Once the bird has imitated the first word, it will soon learn more. If your Grey Parrot is especially talented, then it is impossible to teach it something specific, because it will spontaneously imitate everything it hears in its environment. It could also turn out that the "joker" will repeat everything except what you want to hear. This can, however, lead to some of the funniest situations.

Some Grey Parrots

Never grab your Grey Parrot with your hands to do unpleasant tasks such as filing the nails or clipping the wings. It is better that the bird not associate the experience with your hands. Photo by Louise Van der Meid.

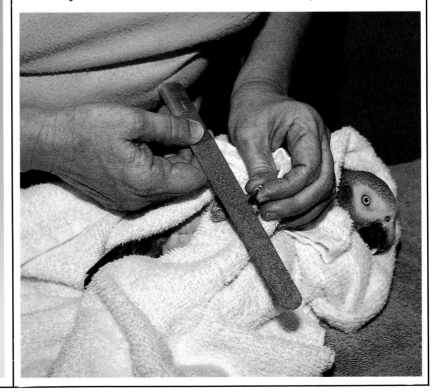

condition of the sprouted seed, and only an amount that the birds can eat in three to four hours should be fed. In order to meet the increased calcium and mineral requirements of the breeding pair, plenty of cuttlebone should be supplied.

COURTSHIP AND BREEDING BEHAVIOR

Courtship behavior is not very pronounced in Grey Parrots and differs from individual to individual. Courting birds often run with drooping wings back and forth on the perches, and in so doing occasionally pause to scratch each other's heads. With birds inclined to breed, the male often feeds its mate; it "practices," so to speak, for later, when it must provide the incubating female and the youngsters with food.

The female lays two to five eggs at intervals of two to four days. The female usually starts incubating after the first egg is laid, and the youngsters hatch at corresponding intervals. The birds should not be disturbed during this time if possible, because even hand-tamed Grey Parrots act aggressively toward their provider in the course of their breeding activity.

Ten day old Grey Parrot chicks. The Grey Parrot has a very rapid growth rate. At this age the chicks are receiving feedings every 3 hours. Photo by Louise Van der Meid.

Opposite:
Young Grey
Parrots
learn to
mimic
quicker than
adult birds.
They also
comprehend
things faster
and speak
more than
adults.
Photo by
Robert
Pearcy.

During the 29-to-31-day incubation period, the females sit very tightly on the eggs and often lose a part of their belly plumage. During this time females are fed from the males' crops.

THE OFFSPRING

The newly hatched youngsters are almost bare and have only isolated hair-like down. After two weeks, the new arrival is already well-covered with down, and toward the end of the fourth week of life, the first feathers begin to grow. After six to seven weeks, the head and wings are feathered and the first red tail feathers appear. The nestling period lasts about three months, until the first youngster leaves the nest cavity after hatching. During the entire time the young Grey Parrots are fed by their parents. At first, the female clasps the still-straight bill of the youngster with its own bill and turns it around in such a way that its head is in a favorable position for feeding. A few days later, the little bird can already lift its head without assistance. Eight to ten days after the first young Grey Parrot hatches, the male also begins to provide the youngsters, which cry like tiny kittens, with food from its crop.

In the last weeks prior to leaving the nest, the female no longer sleeps in the nest box. The fledged youngsters continue to be fed by the parents, and slowly learn from the adults how to eat seeds and other foods. They become truly independent in the sixth month of life.

HAND-REARING

With Grey Parrots, hand-rearing is becoming more popular, it used to be a last resort, when there was no other way to keep the youngsters alive because of an accident or a lack of parental care. They should be fed a high protein hand-feeding formula that can be purchased from a private breeder or pet shop. The formula should be mixed with a small animal multivitamin supplement, and is fed directly into the bill using a pipette with a funnel-shaped enlargement in the front or a syringe. Larger youngsters can be fed with a small plastic spoon. The danger is greater that a youngster will starve from lack of food than having been overfed. It requires a great deal of patience to acclimate a little Grey Parrot to this unnatural method of food intake and to rear it.

Illnesses

Opposite:
Perches
should be of
various
thickness so
that the
parrots feet
are
exercised.
Photo by
Robert
Pearcy.

GENERAL HEALTH CARE AND ILLNESSES

Well-acclimated Grey Parrots are not delicate birds and if given proper care, seldom become ill. However, new acquisitions, particularly hand raised animals, are susceptible to illnesses because their immune systems are not completely built up.

In the following pages, the most common illnesses and minor indispositions are described. If your bird seems to be listless or seriously ill—typical symptoms are diarrhea, difficulty in breathing, lack of appetite, dull plumage, or swollen eyes—you should definitely call in a veterinarian who is experienced with birds.

COLDS

Even the healthiest parrot can sneeze once in a while, but a persistent cold is always serious. If a newly acquired animal exhibits cold symptoms, the patient should first be moved to a warm place. Warmth is a "proven home remedy" with all sick tropical birds. Hang a heat lamp over the cage in such a way that the bird can leave the illuminated area at any time. The temperature can safely be maintained at 35–40°C (95–104°F). Nostrils encrusted with mucus should be daubed clean with a weak solution (5 percent) of table salt. If there is a noticeable difficulty in breathing, a veterinarian should be consulted.

INFLAMMATIONS OF THE EYES OR LACHRYMAL GLANDS

Eye inflammations can be recognized by gummed-up eyelids

The sense of smell in birds is so great that they usually will not drink or eat something that has medication or vitamins added to it. Photo by Michael Gilroy.

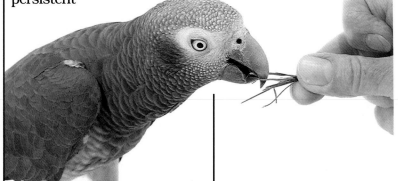

and scabby deposits, and are principally caused by bacterial infection. A vitamin-A deficiency can promote these inflammations. They can also be caused by an ornithosis infection. They are treated with antibiotic eye salves (for example, aureomycin eye salve). A swelling over the eye that remains after an inflammation fades away can be removed by the veterinarian by means of a minor surgical procedure.

DIARRHEA

Diarrhea brought about by a change in diet and stress can usually be cured by feeding the parrot cooked rice and spring water. Nothing else should be given to it during this period.

MOLT

A molt in the sense that the entire plumage is replaced all at once does not occur with Grey Parrots. The feathers are replaced continuously. Occasionally the remnants of clipped flight feathers are not shed and new feathers cannot grow back in the affected places. In this case, a veterinarian should remove the sheaths of the old feathers.

FEATHER PLUCKING OR FEATHER EATING

This disturbance, which mainly occurs in singly kept Grey Parrots, primarily has psychological causes. At first the birds usually pluck the feathers from the breast. Later on, feathers are also torn out on other parts of the body, so that eventually the bird is bare except for the head and wings. Here a change in living conditions can help, such as a new environment or activity, or the company of others of its kind.

In 1959 the author was shown a Grey Parrot that had feathers only on the head and wings. The feather plucking had been triggered by the recently begun business activity of its provider, who now could not spend as much time with the bird. The patient's flight feathers were clipped and it was placed in a new environment. Because it was a warm summer, the bird was able to live outdoors for months. Wild birds provided a diversion, and the parrot was fully occupied. By fall, all of the feathers had grown back. The owner then bought a second Grey Parrot, and since then this bird has not plucked any more feathers. During the entire time, no change in diet was made,

which is proof that feather plucking is not always attributed to dietary, physiological causes.

CROP CONSTIPATION

Spoiled or poisonous food (for example, rancid sunflower seeds) causes an abnormal swelling of the crop in the afflicted bird. Treatment is carried out with cooked rice, to which a little lemon juice is added. Before the Grey Parrot receives this food, it should go 24 hours without eating. If there is no improvement, a veterinarian must be consulted because crop constipation must be surgically treated in an emergency. In order to prevent a chronic inflammatory condition, antibiotics and cortisone are administered by the veterinarian after an operation.

ORNITHOSIS

This illness, which is also called psittacosis (parrot fever), is certainly rare in Grey Parrots, but can never be ruled out with 100% certainty even after a lawfully conducted quarantine. The illness by no means affects only parrots, but, on the contrary, infects many other species of birds as well. When birds are kept outdoors, it is possible for the infection to be transmitted through wild birds (for example, sparrows and pigeons). Because ornithosis can also infect people, every bird owner should be familiar with the course of illness. Today, the pathogen is classified with the bacteria under the name Chlamydia ornithosis; in older literature, ornithosis was still included with the viral illnesses. A complete spectrum of symptoms can occur, from slight cold symptoms to serious inflammations of the respiratory and digestive organs. Eye inflammations are not rare. The pathogen is shed with the droppings, and, after they dry out, is transmitted further with the dust. Infections through droplets produced by sneezing are also possible. Infected birds suffer from difficulty in breathing and persistent cold and shivers, often accompanied by a slimy, yellowish green diarrhea. With proper treatment, almost all infected birds can be saved with broad-spectrum antibiotics. Because a sure diagnosis requires a serological test, the treatment of this notifiable illness is carried out by a veterinarian. Any

use of the prescribed antibiotics (aureomycin, tetracycline, chloramphenicol, and so forth) must take place only in the manner and dosage prescribed by the veterinarian. Because infected birds eat very little, the Psittacin in pellet form used as a prophylactic during the quarantine period is only of limited value.

In human beings, ornithosis infection generally appears in an influenza-like form, and can lead up to serious illnesses like pneumonia and pleurisy. People who regularly come in contact with birds should always alert the treating physician to the possibility of an ornithosis infection.

SALMONELLOSIS AND COLIBACILLOSIS

In both cases, it is a question of infectious bacterial diseases that occur in birds kept outdoors. Salmonella pathogens are transmitted through the droppings of mice and rats and infected wild birds. In contrast to this, the pathogen of colibacillosis—*Escherichia*

Adolescent birds are more susceptible to illness than adults. Their immune systems are not completely built up and it is best to be extra careful of drafts and other birds that it may come into contact with. Photo by Joan Balzarini.

coli—normally lives in the intestines of birds and triggers an illness only under specific conditions; for example, stress. The consequences are diarrhea, ruffled plumage, and reduced food intake. A diagnosis is only possible through the bacterial examination of a specimen's droppings. Treatment occurs with tetracycline or chloramphenicol under a veterinarian's supervision.

ASPERGILLOSIS

Aspergillosis should always be suspected if antibiotic treatments are ineffective for infections of the respiratory tract. This is a dangerous illness, which is caused by fungi of the genus *Aspergillus*. This fungus is particularly prevalent in the late summer months under suitable conditions of humidity and temperature. Already weakened parrots and youngsters are especially susceptible to becoming infected through inhaled fungal spores, which then become established in the air passages and begin to grow there. The result is difficulty in breathing, which in serious cases is expressed in a rhythmic opening and closing of the bill. Until recently, one was

helpless against this insidious disease. In the meantime, repeated successful treatments through a miconazol medicine originating from human medicine have been reported.

THRUSH

Another fungal disease is thrush, which is caused by an infection with the yeast fungus *Candida albicans*. This organism can occur, for example, in bad or spoiled food. *Candida* infections often give rise to crop inflammations. The infection is treated according to the veterinarian's prescription.

PARASITIC INFESTATION

Mites and feather mites (*Mallophaga*) injure the skin and plumage. It is safest to control them with a pure pyrethrum medication. Pyrethrum is a highly effective toxin against parasites which is isolated from plants and is not dangerous for warmblooded animals. When dusting the bird with it, you must be sure that the eyes and nostrils are protected from the powder.

MANGE MITES

These microscopic mites attack the horn-covered parts of the feet. They are

extremely rare in Grey Parrots. The infestation shows up as an itching irritation: the bird scratches and rubs the affected areas. A sure diagnosis is possible only by means of microscopic examination of skin and horn specimens. The condition is treated with thin, oily or spirit-based lotions, malathion, monosulfiram, sulphur in oil and many others can also be used.

WORM INFESTATION

In birds kept in outdoor aviaries, threadworms (*Capillarians*) and roundworms (*Ascarids*) can occur. These parasites are all host specific (that is, they attack specific kinds of birds) and cannot be transmitted to humans. A worm infestation can manifest itself in enteritis and diarrhea; however, the bird can be infested with worms even if it appears to be completely healthy. Often the worm infestation will become evident only if the bird has already been

It is always best to watch for signs that indicate an oncoming illness. Any change in your bird's behavior or eating habits should be guarded carefully. Photo by Michael Gilroy.

The eyes of a healthy bird always appear bright and clear. Photo by Michael Gilroy.

weakened by other stress factors or illnesses.

If a worm infestation is suspected, dropping specimens are sent to a parasitological laboratory (the address can be obtained from any veterinarian). Only when the dropping specimens yield a positive result is a worm cure undertaken according to prescription. A scrupulously thorough disinfection of the cage, climbing tree or aviary (including seed/water dishes and perches) is then particularly important.

POISONINGS

Here the precaution, "an ounce of prevention is better than a pound of cure," is especially important because poisonings often cannot be treated. All kinds of cleaning agents, paint solvents, and insecticides are dangerous. Most often, however, parrots injure themselves by chewing on poisonous house plants: the wax plant (*Hoya carnosa*), oleander (*Nerium oleander*), nux vomica (*Strychnos nux-vomica*), periwinkle (*Vinca minor*), and all species of the genus *Dieffenbachia* should not be placed within reach of the parrot!

FRACTURES AND INJURIES

The treatment of bone fractures and large wounds should be left to a veterinarian. Small wounds should be sterilized with a wound-disinfecting solution and then sprinkled with an antibiotic powder.

ADMINISTERING MEDICINES

Determine your Grey Parrot's weight before calling or visiting the veterinarian. The veterinarian can then calculate the dosage of the required medicine on the basis of the weight. It is recommended to hide bitter pills in a small quantity of a treat so that everything is eaten. If medicines must be administered orally, the bird should be held in its natural perching position and should not be turned on its back. Packing the medicine in a pea-sized piece of butter that rapidly melts in the parrot's mouth and is swallowed can also be helpful. If medicines are mixed in the drinking water, the Grey Parrot should be given only dry food. Liquid medicines are administered by drops directly into the bill. In addition, medications can be injected by the veterinarian or conveyed directly into the crop by means of a probe.

SUGGESTED READING

T.F.H. offers the most comprehensive selections of books dealing with pet birds. A selection of significant titles is presented here; they and the thousands of other animal books published by T.F.H. are available at the same place you bought this one, or write to us for a free catalog.

Index

Page numbers in boldface refer to illustrations.